I0426247

April 2012

RENEWABLE ENERGY PROJECT FINANCING

Improved Guidance and Information Sharing Needed for DOD Project-Level Officials

GAO
Accountability ★ Integrity ★ Reliability

GAO-12-401

RENEWABLE ENERGY PROJECT FINANCING

Improved Guidance and Information Sharing Needed for DOD Project-Level Officials

GAO
Accountability * Integrity * Reliability

Highlights

Highlights of GAO-12-401, a report to congressional committees

Why GAO Did This Study

DOD is the largest consumer of energy in the federal government, spending about $3.8 billion on facilities' energy at more than 500 permanent military installations throughout the world in fiscal year 2010. The House Armed Services Committee directed GAO to review issues related to financing approaches for renewable energy projects on military installations. GAO (1) determined the approaches that military services are using to finance renewable energy projects and the factors the services consider in selecting an approach, (2) assessed the extent to which the services have established methods to obtain good value and advantageous contract terms and manage risks of financing approaches for renewable energy projects, and (3) identified the extent to which the services developed guidance, training, and other resources to assist officials in selecting and implementing financing approaches.

GAO reviewed applicable legal authorities, guidance, and project information from selected projects and interviewed officials from the Office of the Secretary of Defense, military services, 10 selected installations, and the Department of Energy.

What GAO Recommends

GAO recommends that DOD issue comprehensive guidance to ensure key analyses are completed and available-financing approaches are fully considered. GAO also recommends that DOD develop a formalized communications process to share best practices on financing renewable energy projects among installations. DOD generally concurred with GAO's recommendations.

View GAO-12-401. For more information, contact Brian J. Lepore at (202) 512-4523 or leporeb@gao.gov or Frank Rusco at (202) 512-3841 or ruscof@gao.gov.

What GAO Found

To finance renewable energy projects, the military services use up-front appropriations, such as operation and maintenance funds, and alternative-financing approaches that generally rely on private capital, such as arranging financing and implementing a project with a private developer or utility. The military services have funded about 85 percent of nearly 600 projects that were in design, under construction, or operating in fiscal year 2011 with up-front appropriations, but financed 8 of the 9 large-scale projects and 19 of the 57 medium-scale projects with alternative financing. Several factors affect the military services' use of financing approaches, including perceived benefits and drawbacks such as how long it takes to obtain funding.

The military services have established methods to help ensure good value and advantageous contract terms and to manage the risks of the various financing approaches, but the services have not issued comprehensive guidance on how and when to prepare analyses for renewable energy projects. For example, headquarters and installation officials said that military services use business case or other cost analyses to help maximize benefits and mitigate drawbacks of the selected financing approach. However, GAO found examples of installations' not developing cost analyses or not analyzing different financing approaches for projects, as well as uncertainty about how to account for some benefits in the analyses, because the military services generally do not have guidance to ensure that business case analyses are completed and that analyses fully consider the costs and benefits of different financing approaches. As a result of not having processes and comprehensive guidance in place, the military services cannot ensure that decision makers select the financing approach that maximizes benefits and mitigates drawbacks or risks of available financing approaches.

The Department of Defense (DOD) and other agencies have made available guidance, training, and other resources to assist officials in selecting certain financing approaches for renewable energy projects, but some guidance on the approaches is inconsistent and information sharing at the installation level is ad hoc and not formalized. DOD, the Department of Energy, and the military services have developed an increasing amount of guidance on the available financing approaches; however, GAO found instances where different interpretations of some guidance affected the approaches the services used because DOD has not issued overarching guidance on using these approaches. As a result, the military services may not be taking full advantage of the various approaches available to finance projects to meet renewable energy goals. Additionally, DOD personnel were generally satisfied with training they received on the financing approaches, but DOD does not have a formalized process to share information and best practices on the approaches among project-level officials across the military services at the installation level. As a result, DOD cannot ensure that officials responsible for selecting a financing approach have timely access on an ongoing basis to information on approaches that their counterparts from other services have used and their experiences with those approaches. Such information could assist the officials in selecting a financing approach that maximizes the benefits and minimizes the drawbacks or risks of that approach.

_____ United States Government Accountability Office

Contents

Tables

Figures

Abbreviations

DOD	Department of Defense
ECIP	Energy Conservation Investment Program
ESPC	Energy Savings Performance Contract
EUL	enhanced-use lease
PPA	power purchase agreement
UESC	Utility Energy Service Contract

United States Government Accountability Office
Washington, DC 20548

April 4, 2012

Congressional Committees

The Department of Defense (DOD) is the largest consumer of energy in the federal government. DOD reported spending $15.2 billion on all types of energy in fiscal year 2010, with about 25 percent of this amount—or about $3.8 billion—spent on energy for facilities at more than 500 permanent military installations throughout the world, and the remaining amount spent on the energy used for training, moving, and sustaining military forces and weapons platforms for military operations.[1] In addition to the cost of energy, DOD reported in 2011 that its dependence on the commercial electricity grid for facilities' energy leaves the department vulnerable to service disruptions and places the continuity of critical missions at risk. As such, DOD's strategy for facilities' energy management seeks to, among other actions, increase the supply of renewable and alternative energy sources and improve energy security by addressing the threat of commercial grid disruption with on-site generation capacity.[2] Along with providing energy security, DOD reported that developing renewable energy on military installations can help DOD reduce its reliance on fossil fuels. According to the Department of Energy's Energy Information Administration, fossil fuels are used to generate most of the electricity in the United States, with about 45 percent of the more than 4 trillion kilowatt hours of electricity produced in

---

[1]Department of Defense, Office of the Deputy Under Secretary of Defense (Installations and Environment), *Department of Defense Annual Energy Management Report Fiscal Year 2010* (Washington, D.C.: July 2011).

[2]Energy security for DOD means having assured access to reliable supplies of energy and the ability to protect and deliver sufficient energy to meet operational needs. We have previously reported that because certain renewable energy technologies, such as solar and wind, provide intermittent power, they require expensive batteries to store the energy they produce or supplementary, conventional generation to ensure uninterrupted power. GAO, *Defense Infrastructure: DOD Needs to Take Actions to Address Challenges in Meeting Federal Renewable Energy Goals*, GAO-10-104 (Washington, D.C.: Dec. 18, 2009).

2010 generated from coal, about 24 percent from natural gas, and about 1 percent from petroleum.[3]

We have previously reported on DOD's facilities energy efforts. In our December 2009 report, we found that DOD faces challenges in meeting federal renewable energy goals.[4] Among other challenges, we reported that renewable energy is often more expensive than nonrenewable energy and using renewable energy can be at odds with DOD and Department of Energy guidance that calls for DOD to invest in energy projects when cost-effective. These higher costs are because of the relatively high up-front capital costs of renewable energy technologies and the fact that some sources operate intermittently, which results in less energy generated compared to the equipment's energy-generation capacity. For example, solar energy can be generated only during daytime hours and wind energy can be generated only during periods of sustained wind activity. Additionally, we issued a report in April 2010 that identified the department's renewable energy projects that were producing energy or under development at that time, the costs of each of DOD's renewable energy initiatives, and the goals of each of the initiatives.[5]

In a report accompanying a bill for the National Defense Authorization Act for Fiscal Year 2012 (H.R. 1540),[6] the House Armed Services Committee noted that alternatively financed projects—which generally rely on private capital—can be of great benefit to DOD, but expressed concern that project-level officials may not have the necessary information to develop contracts that most effectively leverage a variety of factors, including resource potential, federal and state incentives, payback periods, state regulations, and other regulatory considerations. The Committee directed us to review a number of issues related to financing approaches used for

---

[3]U.S. Energy Information Administration, *Electric Power Annual 2010* (December 2011). In 2010, nuclear power was used to generate about 20 percent of the country's electricity, with hydropower and other renewable sources comprising about 10 percent.

[4]GAO-10-104.

[5]GAO, *Defense Infrastructure: Department of Defense Renewable Energy Initiatives*, GAO-10-681R (Washington, D.C.: Apr. 26, 2010).

[6]H.R. Rep. No. 112-78.

renewable energy projects on military installations.[7] Based on this congressional direction, we (1) determined the approaches that the military services are using to finance renewable energy projects on military installations and the factors that the services consider in selecting a financing approach, (2) assessed the extent to which the military services have established methods to obtain "good value and advantageous contract terms" for renewable energy projects on installations and maximize benefits and mitigate drawbacks or risks of financing approaches,[8] and (3) identified the extent to which the military services have developed guidance, training, and other resources to assist officials in selecting and implementing financing approaches for renewable energy projects.

To determine the approaches the military services are using to finance renewable energy projects on military installations, we compared applicable legal authorities—identified through a legal review, DOD and Department of Energy guidance, training materials, and previous GAO reports—to the financing approaches that DOD has used for projects that were in design, under construction, or currently operating in fiscal year 2011.[9] Through our data collection and verification process, we found DOD's project data to be sufficiently reliable for the purposes of this

---

[7]Throughout this report, we use the term "financing approaches" to generically refer to projects funded either through up-front appropriations or alternative financing approaches. We define appropriated funding as "up-front" when DOD has been appropriated sufficient funds to pay for the full cost of the renewable energy project before a commitment is made for the project, as opposed to appropriated funds DOD uses to make payments on capital borrowed through certain types of alternative financing approaches. We define "alternative financing" as ways of financing capital assets other than through full, up-front appropriations. We have previously reported that full, up-front appropriations are the best way to maintain governmentwide fiscal control. See GAO, *Budget Issues: Alternative Approaches to Finance Federal Capital*, GAO-03-1011 (Washington, D.C.: Aug. 21, 2003).

[8]For the purposes of this review, we defined the phrase "good value and advantageous contract terms" to mean an acquisition outcome that provides an overall benefit to the government.

[9]For the purposes of this review, we focused on the military services' renewable energy efforts—which comprise the vast majority of DOD's renewable energy projects—and excluded the defense agencies and other defense organizations from our review since they comprise only a small subset of the total number of projects. Additionally, we focused on DOD's efforts to generate renewable energy and excluded from our review nuclear energy and efforts that only addressed energy efficiency or conservation. For more information on the scope of our review, including the definition of renewable energy, see appendix I.

report. To determine the factors that the military services consider when selecting a financing approach for renewable energy projects, including the benefits and drawbacks of each of the financing approaches, we interviewed officials from the Office of the Deputy Under Secretary of Defense (Installations and Environment), the Defense Logistics Agency-Energy office, each of the military service headquarters and their supporting agencies, 10 selected installations, and the Department of Energy. We identified the installations to include in our review by first selecting a nonprobability sample of eight installations—two installations per service—to get a mix of the types of financing approaches used, the types of renewable energy projects implemented, and geographic diversity, with an emphasis on installations that have used multiple financing sources and implemented different types of projects on an individual installation. We then selected two additional installations with unique characteristics to include in our sample. The 10 installations in our sample are Fort Irwin and Marine Corps Air Station Miramar, California; the U.S. Air Force Academy, Colorado; Naval Air Station Jacksonville, Florida; Fort Knox, Kentucky; Nellis Air Force Base, Nevada; Marine Corps Air Station Beaufort, South Carolina; Fort Bliss, Texas; Hill Air Force Base, Utah; and Naval Air Station Oceana, Virginia.

To determine the extent to which the military services have established methods to obtain good value and advantageous contract terms for renewable energy projects on installations and maximize benefits and mitigate risks of financing approaches, we reviewed applicable guidance, directives, and instructions from DOD and the military services related to renewable energy projects. Additionally, we reviewed project documentation for 2 projects at each of the 10 installations included in our scope. We also interviewed officials at the Office of the Deputy Under Secretary of Defense (Installations and Environment), the military service headquarters and their supporting agencies, and the 10 selected installations. Additionally, we reviewed previous GAO reports related to the identified methods to better understand the methods.

To determine the extent to which DOD has developed guidance, training, and other resources to assist officials in selecting and implementing financing approaches for renewable energy projects, we reviewed existing guidance developed by the Under Secretary of Defense (Acquisition, Technology and Logistics) and the military services. We also reviewed information on the training offered through DOD, the Department of Energy, and other sources, such as conferences. Additionally, we spoke with officials at the Office of the Deputy Under Secretary of Defense (Installations and Environment), the Defense

Logistics Agency-Energy office, the military service headquarters and supporting agencies, and the 10 selected installations to determine the availability, quality, and relevance of the guidance, training, and other resources. We also spoke with officials from the Department of Energy's Federal Energy Management Program to discuss the types and quantity of training their agency provides to DOD personnel. For additional information on the scope and methodology of this engagement, see appendix I.

We conducted this performance audit from June 2011 through April 2012, in accordance with generally accepted government auditing standards. Those standards require that we plan and perform the audit to obtain sufficient, appropriate evidence to provide a reasonable basis for our findings and conclusions based on our audit objectives. We believe that the evidence obtained provides a reasonable basis for our findings and conclusions based on our audit objectives.

Background

Renewable Energy Goals

DOD measures its facilities energy performance against federal renewable energy goals. Table 1 lists key laws and an executive order that relate to the consumption or production of renewable energy.

Table 1: Key Federal Goals Related to Renewable Energy

Statute or executive order	Renewable energy-related goal
42 U.S.C. § 15852 (originally enacted in the Energy Policy Act of 2005, Pub. L. No. 109-58, § 203 (2005))	To the extent economically feasible and technically practicable, consume renewable energy equal to at least 3 percent of all electrical energy consumed from fiscal year 2007 to fiscal year 2009, with increases to 5 percent in fiscal year 2010 through fiscal year 2012, and 7.5 percent in fiscal year 2013 and thereafter. The statute also provides additional credit toward these goals for agencies with renewable electricity produced on site subject to certain conditions.
	For the purposes of this goal, the term "renewable energy" means electric energy generated from solar, wind, biomass, landfill gas, ocean (including tidal, wave, current, and thermal), geothermal, municipal solid waste, or new hydroelectric generation capacity achieved from increased efficiency or additions of new capacity at an existing hydroelectric project.
10 USC § 2911(e)	DOD's goal is to produce or procure facility energy from renewable energy sources whenever the use of such renewable energy sources is consistent with the energy performance goals and energy performance master plan for the department and when supported by certain special considerations.
	DOD's goal is also to produce or procure not less than 25 percent of the total quantity of facility energy consumed within its facilities from renewable energy sources during fiscal year 2025 and each fiscal year thereafter.
	For the purposes of these goals, the term "renewable energy source" means energy generated from renewable sources, including: solar; wind; biomass; landfill gas; ocean, including tidal, wave, current, and thermal; geothermal, including electricity and heat pumps; municipal solid waste; new hydroelectric generation capacity achieved from increased efficiency or additions of new capacity at an existing hydroelectric project (for purposes of this subparagraph, hydroelectric generation capacity is "new" if it was placed in service on or after January 1, 1999); thermal energy generated by any of the preceding sources.
Executive Order 13423	Ensure that at least one-half of the statutorily required renewable energy consumed by an agency in a fiscal year comes from "new renewable sources."
	For the purposes of this goal, "new renewable sources" are those sources of renewable energy placed into service after January 1, 1999.

Source: GAO analysis and DOD.

Each of the military services has also established energy goals for the service. The Secretary of the Navy set a goal—among other goals—to derive at least 50 percent of shore-based energy requirements from alternative sources by 2020, which exceeds the federal energy goals listed above. The Army and Air Force set energy goals that are closely tied to the federal goals. Specifically, the Army Energy Security Implementation Strategy established a goal to raise the share of renewable or alternative resources for power and fuel use, noting that this goal also supports federal renewable energy goals.[10] The Air Force Energy Plan expressed a commitment to increasing its available energy supply, including facilities energy, to meet the federal energy goals.[11]

Additionally, DOD and the Department of Energy, as part of a joint effort, have implemented a task force and pilot project to develop a strategy and a process for analyzing the potential for military installations to become "net zero" energy installations—that is, produce as much energy on site or nearby as consumed in the buildings and facilities—and maximize the use of renewable energy resources. The four pilot installations are the United States Air Force Academy, Colorado; the Army's Kahuku Training Area, Hawaii; Marine Corps Air Station Miramar, California; and Naval Support Activity South Potomac, Maryland. In addition to its pilot location, the Army, through its own net zero initiative, identified six additional net zero energy locations and two integrated net zero installations that will be net zero energy, net zero water, and net zero waste.[12] The Secretary of the Navy established a goal to achieve net zero energy at 50 percent of Navy and Marine Corps installations by 2020.

To meet the federal and service-specific energy goals, the military services are implementing a number of projects to generate renewable energy, such as installing solar photovoltaic panels, wind turbines, and biomass projects. In addition to generating renewable energy, DOD is working to reduce energy demand through energy efficiency and conservation measures, such as installing more energy-efficient heating and air-conditioning systems or lighting in its facilities.

---

[10]U.S. Army, *Army Energy Security Implementation Strategy* (Washington D.C.: Jan. 13, 2009).

[11]U.S. Air Force, *Air Force Energy Plan* (Washington, D.C.: 2010).

[12]The Army's six net zero energy locations are Fort Hunter Liggett, Parks Reserve Forces Training Area, and Sierra Army Depot, California; Fort Detrick, Maryland; West Point, New York; and Kwajaelin Atoll, Republic of the Marshall Islands. The Army's two integrated net zero locations are Fort Bliss, Texas, and Fort Carson, Colorado. Integrated net zero installations are comprised of three components: net zero energy, net zero water, and net zero waste. A net zero energy installation produces as much energy on site as it consumes in a year. A net zero water installation limits the consumption of freshwater resources and returns water back to the same watershed so as not to deplete the groundwater and surface water resources of that region in quantity and quality over the course of a year. A net zero waste installation reduces, reuses, and recovers waste streams, converting them to resource values with zero landfill over the course of a year.

Roles of the Office of the Secretary of Defense and the Military Services in DOD's Renewable Energy Activities

The Deputy Under Secretary of Defense (Installations and Environment) is DOD's senior energy official and oversees DOD's implementation of the facilities energy goals described above. The Facilities Energy and Privatization Directorate within the Office of the Deputy Under Secretary of Defense (Installations and Environment) coordinates the DOD facilities energy strategy and related programs.

Within the military services, the offices that oversee installations generally also oversee facilities energy efforts. A number of organizations are also involved in developing and implementing renewable energy projects on the installations, specifically,

- Key offices involved in the Army's facilities' energy efforts include, among others, the Offices of the Assistant Secretary of the Army (Installations, Energy, and Environment), the Deputy Assistant Secretary of the Army (Energy and Sustainability), and the Assistant Chief of Staff for Installation Management; the Installation Management Command; the Energy Initiatives Task Force; and the U.S. Army Corps of Engineers Engineering and Support Center, Huntsville.
- Key offices involved in the Navy's facilities' energy efforts include, among others, the Offices of the Assistant Secretary of the Navy (Energy, Installations, and Environment), the Deputy Assistant Secretary of the Navy (Energy), the Commander, Navy Installations Command, and the Deputy Chief of Naval Operations (Fleet Readiness and Logistics); and the Naval Facilities Engineering Service Center within the Naval Facilities Engineering Command.
- The key office involved in the Marine Corps's facilities' energy efforts is the Office of the Deputy Commandant (Installations and Logistics), among others. The Naval Facilities Engineering Service Center also supports the Marine Corps's energy projects.
- Key offices involved in the Air Force's facilities' energy efforts include, among others, the Offices of the Assistant Secretary of the Air Force (Installations, Environment, and Logistics), the Deputy Assistant Secretary of the Air Force (Energy), and the Air Force Civil Engineer; the Air Force Civil Engineer Support Agency and its Air Force Facility Energy Center; and the Air Force Real Property Agency.

Military Services Use Multiple Approaches to Finance Renewable Energy Projects, and Various Factors Affect the Services' Choices of Approaches

Military Services Use Up-Front Appropriations and Alternative-Financing Approaches to Finance Renewable Energy Projects on Installations

To finance renewable energy projects on military installations, the military services use up-front appropriations, such as operation and maintenance funds or military construction funds, and alternative-financing approaches that generally rely on private capital, such as Energy Savings Performance Contracts or power purchase agreements. Each of the financing approaches has its own requirements and legal authorities. These financing approaches are not necessarily mutually exclusive and different approaches can sometimes be combined to finance the same project. For example, the Army is developing a project at Fort Irwin in which the Army would lease land to a private contractor for up to 50 years through an enhanced-use lease, the developer would build a large solar array on the property, and the installation would purchase energy that is produced by the project through a power purchase agreement. Table 2 provides a summary of selected approaches available to finance renewable energy projects on DOD installations and appendix II provides a more detailed description of these financing approaches and legal authorities.

Table 2: Selected Financing Approaches Available for Acquisition of Renewable Energy or Development of Renewable Energy Projects on DOD Installations

Financing approach	Brief summary of approach	Project examples
Up-front appropriations		
Annual military construction appropriations, including the Energy Conservation Investment Program (ECIP)	The military services can use appropriations for military construction for the acquisition, construction, installation, and equipment of temporary or permanent public works, military installations, facilities, and real property, which can include renewable energy projects. In its annual energy management report, DOD reported spending $6.2 million on 2 renewable energy projects funded with military construction appropriations in fiscal year 2010.[a] The Energy Conservation Investment Program, administered by the Office of the Deputy Under Secretary of Defense (Installations and Environment), is a subset of the Defense-wide Military Construction program specifically designated for projects that save energy or reduce energy costs. In its annual energy management report, DOD reported spending $74.2 million on 32 renewable energy projects funded through the Energy Conservation Investment Program in fiscal year 2010.[a]	Naval Air Station Jacksonville funded a child development center and an integrated training center with military construction appropriations, each of which incorporated solar carports as part of the larger project. Marine Corps Air Station Beaufort funded a barracks building that included a 38.5 kilowatt solar array as part of the larger project. The barracks building is under construction and expected to be completed in 2012. Marine Corps Air Station Miramar installed a solar carport, generating 260 kilowatts, and is installing a second, generating 300 kilowatts, using appropriated funds through the Energy Conservation Investment Program.
Operation and maintenance appropriations	The military services can use operation and maintenance appropriations for certain small military construction projects (limited to projects costing less than $750,000), which could include renewable energy projects, and certain repairs and renovations, which could include energy efficiencies or other energy-related repairs. The military services fund some renewable energy projects using operation and maintenance funds that are managed by the installation. Additionally, the Navy, Marine Corps, and Air Force have funded renewable energy projects with operation and maintenance funds that are managed centrally at the headquarters level. In its annual energy management report, DOD reported spending nearly $17 million on 64 renewable energy projects funded with operation and maintenance appropriations in fiscal year 2010.[a]	The U.S. Air Force Academy installed ground source heat pumps at several locations that were funded through installation-managed operation and maintenance funds. One project was for a guard house that was not located near a gas line so, according to installation officials, the heat pumps were the most cost-effective way to heat and cool the facility. Nellis Air Force Base installed solar photovoltaic panels to power the installation's marquee sign, which was paid for, in part, with the Air Force's centrally managed operation and maintenance funds.

Financing approach	Brief summary of approach	Project examples
Other up-front appropriations	Periodically, Congress makes available other direct appropriations that can be used for renewable energy projects. For example, DOD reported spending nearly $200 million of appropriated funds from the American Recovery and Reinvestment Act of 2009 on renewable energy projects. DOD has also used appropriated funds programmed for the Environmental Security Technology Certification Program, DOD's environmental technology demonstration and validation program, to fund renewable energy projects on DOD installations.	Fort Irwin replaced more than 300 street lights with solar street lights using appropriated funding from the American Recovery and Reinvestment Act of 2009. DOD is installing a demonstration project at the U.S. Air Force Academy, which was funded through the Environmental Security Technology Certification Program and is expected to be placed into service in 2012. In this project, dining hall food waste will be used in an anaerobic digestion process to produce methane gas, which produces renewable energy. The project will test which nutrients increase the digestion process.
Alternative-financing approaches		
Energy Savings Performance Contract (ESPC)	An Energy Savings Performance Contract is a contract between a federal agency and an energy service provider. Based on the results of a comprehensive energy audit, an energy service company, in consultation with the federal agency, designs and constructs a project to save energy and arranges the necessary financing. The contractor guarantees that the improvements will generate energy cost savings sufficient to pay for the project over the term of the contract. Contract terms for Energy Savings Performance Contracts can extend up to 25 years. In its annual energy management report, DOD reported that the department awarded 22 projects through Energy Savings Performance Contracts totaling $277 million in fiscal year 2010; however, most of these were energy efficiency, not renewable energy, projects.[a]	Naval Air Station Oceana implemented a number of ground source heat pump projects that service more than 1.5 million square feet of facilities, including some projects financed through Energy Savings Performance Contracts. Hill Air Force Base financed a landfill gas-to-energy project with a total capacity of 2.3 megawatts through an Energy Savings Performance Contract. Fort Bliss financed a solar thermal system to heat a swimming pool—among other energy conservation measures—through an Energy Savings Performance Contract.
Utility Energy Service Contract (UESC)	In a Utility Energy Service Contract, a utility arranges financing to cover the capital costs of a project, which are repaid by the agency, generally using appropriated funds, over the contract term. Repayments are usually based on estimated cost savings generated by the energy efficiency measures, but energy savings are not necessarily required to be guaranteed by the contractor. In its annual energy management report, DOD reported that the department awarded 14 projects through Utility Energy Service Contracts totaling $46 million in fiscal year 2010; however, most of these were energy efficiency projects.[a]	Naval Air Station Jacksonville financed a solar thermal heating project for the Navy Bureau of Medicine and Surgery pool and a solar-powered entrance sign through Utility Energy Service Contracts. Fort Knox financed a 1.8-kilowatt wind turbine through a Utility Energy Service Contract.

Financing approach	Brief summary of approach	Project examples
Power purchase agreement (PPA)	Power purchase agreements for renewable energy may take several forms, but all are essentially agreements to purchase renewable energy from a private-sector energy producer. For example, in some of these agreements, the developer installs a renewable energy-system on agency property, and the agency pays for the system through its purchase of power over the life of the contract. After installation, the developer owns, operates, and maintains the system for the life of the contract. DOD refers to power purchase agreements undertaken using certain authorities as Energy Services Contracts. Depending on the authority used, DOD can enter into power purchase agreements for up to 32 years, excluding the period for construction.	Nellis Air Force Base purchases electricity generated by the 14 megawatt solar array owned by a private contractor and located on the installation. Marine Corps Air Station Miramar plans to purchase three megawatts of electricity generated by landfill gas from a contractor. The landfill is located on Navy property leased to the City of San Diego.
Enhanced-use lease (EUL)[b]	An enhanced-use lease allows the military services to outlease available nonexcess real property to the private sector in return for cash or in-kind consideration, subject to certain conditions. Enhanced-use leases have been used for a wide range of facility improvement projects, renovations, repair, or new acquisitions, to include renewable energy projects. The length of a contract for an enhanced-use lease is subject to certain conditions, but there is no firm time limit. We have previously reported that these leases are often entered into for long periods, such as 25- or 50-year terms.	The Army is currently developing a project at Fort Irwin in which the Army would lease land to a contractor to build a 500-megawatt solar array.
Convey utility system to a utility company	In this approach the secretary of a military department may convey existing utility systems owned by DOD to a utility company in exchange for compensation. One type of contemplated compensation is provision of power at reduced rates. Contracts for provision of power in exchange for conveyance of a utility system are limited to 10 years or, subject to certain conditions, up to 50 years.	According to military service officials, the services have not used this authority for renewable energy projects on military installations.
Sell electricity to a utility	This approach involves the secretary of a military department selling certain kinds of electricity generated on a military installation to a utility (subject to certain requirements) and depositing the proceeds in the appropriation account available to the relevant military department for the supply of electrical energy. Those funds may be used (under certain conditions) to finance certain energy related military construction projects.	The Navy used this authority for its geothermal plant at Naval Air Weapons Station China Lake, California. According to military service officials, the Army, Marine Corps, and Air Force have not used this authority for renewable energy projects on military installations.

Financing approach	Brief summary of approach	Project examples
Lease-to-own energy production facilities	This approach involves the secretary of a military department entering into an agreement with a private sector entity to "lease-to-own" certain facilities provided at the expense of the contractor on a military installation. At the end of the lease, title to the property would vest in the United States. This approach can be used for a variety of facilities, including energy production facilities. Contract terms may not exceed 32 years.	According to military service officials, the services have not used this authority for renewable energy projects on military installations.

Source: GAO analysis of approaches and legal authorities.

Note: We did not include in our analysis certain other approaches that could potentially be available to DOD for the financing of renewable energy projects, such as approaches that could only be employed in narrowly defined situations or that may not be useful departmentwide. For example, we excluded 10 U.S.C. § 2686, which authorizes the secretary of a military department to sell or contract to sell certain specific utilities (including electrical power) to purchasers in the immediate vicinity of an activity of the relevant service under certain unusual circumstances (e.g. the utility is not otherwise available from a local source).

[a]Office of the Deputy Under Secretary of Defense (Installations and Environment), *Department of Defense Annual Energy Management Report, Fiscal Year 2010* (Washington, D.C.: July 2011).

[b]The military services refer to certain leases of real property undertaken pursuant to the authority in 10 U.S.C. § 2667 as "enhanced-use leases."

The military services have varied in their use of up-front appropriations and alternative-financing approaches for renewable energy projects on military installations. Based on our analysis of DOD's data on renewable energy projects, of the nearly 600 projects that were in design, under construction, or currently operating in fiscal year 2011, the military services funded about 85 percent of the projects with up-front appropriations. Table 3 shows the number of renewable energy projects the military services identified as being in design, under construction, or currently operating in fiscal year 2011 and the financing approaches used for the projects.

Table 3: Financing Approaches Used for Renewable Energy Projects and Number of Projects in Design, under Construction, or Currently Operating on Military Installations in Fiscal Year 2011

Financing approach	Army	Navy	Marine Corps	Air Force	Total
Up-front appropriations	158[a]	160	71	120[b]	**509**
Annual military construction appropriations[c]	42	19	7	19	**87**
Energy Conservation Investment Program[c]	29	38	26	21[b]	**114[b]**
Operation and maintenance appropriations	41[a]	57	32	64[b]	**194 [a, b]**
American Recovery and Reinvestment Act of 2009	27	34	4	8	**73**
Other up-front appropriations	20[a, d]	12	2	9	**43[a]**
Alternative financing	26	23	20	19	**88**
Energy Savings Performance Contract	15	10	5	8	**38**
Utility Energy Service Contract	8	10	13	3	**34**
Power purchase agreement	2	1	1	7	**11**
Enhanced-use lease	1	0	0	1	**2**
Other alternative-financing approaches	0	2[e]	1[f]	0	**3**
Total (all projects)	**184**	**183**	**91**	**139**	**597**

Source: GAO analysis of DOD data.

Notes: According to military service officials, installations may have additional renewable energy projects operating on the installation that are not included in these figures. According to the officials, these are often smaller projects, such as a solar panel or ground source heat pump on a single building, that are funded through installation-managed operation and maintenance funds and are not reviewed or approved by the military service headquarters. Therefore, the headquarters officials may not be aware of the projects.

There may be differences between the data provided to us by the military services above and the data reported by DOD in its annual energy management report because DOD only reports the projects that are currently producing renewable energy and we reported on projects that were in design or under construction in fiscal year 2011, in addition to those that were already producing renewable energy in fiscal year 2011.

[a]One Army project was funded with a combination of operation and maintenance funds and other up-front appropriations. We listed this project in both rows, but only counted the project once in the overall totals.

[b]One Air Force project was funded with a combination of up-front appropriations from the operation and maintenance account and the Energy Conservation Investment Program. We listed this project in both rows, but only counted the project once in the overall totals.

[c]Projects included in the annual military construction appropriations row do not include projects funded through the Energy Conservation Investment Program.

[d]The Army could not provide information on the specific source of up-front appropriations for five projects. Therefore, we included these projects in the "other up-front appropriations" category.

[e]The Navy could not provide information on the specific alternative-financing approach used for two projects. Therefore, we included these projects in the "other alternative financing approaches" category.

[f]The Marine Corps could not provide information on the approach used to finance one project, but an official noted that it was not funded with up-front appropriations allocated by Marine Corps Headquarters. Therefore, we included this project in the "other alternative-financing approaches" category.

The majority of the military services' renewable energy projects—531 of 597 projects, or almost 90 percent—are small-scale projects, designed to produce less than 1,000-megawatt hours of energy annually.[13] The services paid for almost 90 percent of these small-scale projects with up-front appropriations. Small-scale projects include such things as solar panels or ground source heat pumps on individual buildings. The services have developed or implemented nine large-scale projects, each designed to produce more than 50,000-megawatt hours of energy annually. The services financed eight of the nine large-scale projects with alternative-financing approaches. These large-scale projects include a biogenic methane gas project at Fort Knox, financed through a Utility Energy Service Contract, and a 500-megawatt solar project currently in design at Edwards Air Force Base, California. Finally, the services have developed or implemented 57 medium-scale projects, each designed to produce between 1,000- and 49,999-megawatt hours of energy annually. The services funded 38 projects, or two-thirds of these medium-scale projects, with up-front appropriations and the remaining one-third with alternative-financing approaches. These medium-scale projects include ground source heat pumps at Marine Corps Air Station Beaufort, financed through an Energy Savings Performance Contract; and wind turbines at F.E. Warren Air Force Base, Wyoming, financed through up-front appropriations from the Energy Conservation Investment Program.

Use of Financing Approaches Is Affected by Various Factors

The decision to use a specific financing approach, whether up-front appropriations or alternative financing, is dependent on a number of factors, including the benefits and drawbacks or risks of the specific approach and the limitations of some financing approaches. Officials we interviewed from the Office of the Deputy Under Secretary of Defense (Installations and Environment), military services' headquarters, selected military installations, and the Department of Energy identified a number of benefits and drawbacks or risks of the financing approaches for renewable energy projects. Appendix III provides a summary of the benefits and drawbacks or risks that these officials identified. In several cases, the benefits and drawbacks or risks present trade-offs for decision makers to consider in selecting a financing approach. Key issues and trade-offs that the officials identified include:

---

[13]To put this in context, according to the Department of Energy's Energy Information Administration, the average American household used nearly 11,500-kilowatt hours (or 11.5-megawatt hours) of electricity in 2010.

- *Up-front appropriations versus long-term finance charges.* Some officials mentioned the length of time it can take to navigate the programming and budgeting process and to obtain appropriations as a drawback to using the up-front appropriated funding approaches for renewable energy projects. Specifically, some officials stated that it can take three to five years from project submission within the service through beginning construction for projects funded through military construction appropriations—including the Energy Conservation Investment Program—because of the length of the budget and appropriations cycle. In contrast, when financing a renewable energy project with an alternative-financing approach, the installation can pay back the costs over time while obtaining the benefit of the project—such as renewable energy production—almost immediately after the project is constructed. However, several officials noted that paying for the project using an alternative-financing approach often leads to a costlier project in the long term when compared to the same project paid for using up-front appropriated funding because of the cost of private financing. We have previously reported that alternative-financing approaches may be more expensive over time than full, up-front appropriations since the federal government's cost of capital is lower than that of the private sector.[14]

- *Operation and maintenance of equipment.* According to several officials, the operation and maintenance of equipment is a benefit of most alternatively financed projects and a drawback of projects funded with up-front appropriations. Projects financed with an alternative-financing approach generally involve the contractor operating and maintaining the equipment during the contract period, whereas the government typically is responsible for the operation and maintenance of equipment purchased with appropriated funds. Officials cited this as a significant benefit of alternatively financed projects—and a drawback of projects funded with up-front appropriations—because, according to the officials, installations often do not have personnel on-staff with the knowledge, skills, or expertise to operate and maintain the equipment needed to generate renewable energy. Officials noted, however, that for projects financed with Energy Savings Performance Contracts or Utility Energy Service Contracts, the contract period could be a relatively short period of time. According to these officials, after the contract period ends, the

---

[14]GAO, *Capital Financing: Partnerships and Energy Savings Performance Contracts Raise Budgeting and Monitoring Concerns*, GAO-05-55 (Washington, D.C.: Dec. 16, 2004).

installation assumes ownership—and therefore the operation and maintenance—of the equipment, which can be a drawback of these two approaches.

- *Availability of funding.* Some military service headquarters and installation officials said that, in recent years, they have preferred to use up-front appropriations to pay for renewable energy projects on installations since an increased amount of appropriated funding has been available for such projects through the American Recovery and Reinvestment Act of 2009, the Energy Conservation Investment Program, and centrally managed operation and maintenance funding from the military services. However, officials said that they expect they will need to seek alternative financing for renewable energy projects in the future due to likely reductions in the availability of up-front appropriated funding. Some officials noted that a drawback of each of the appropriated fund sources is that renewable energy projects must compete with other projects for funding and renewable energy projects are often a lower priority than other projects because of the relatively higher cost and lower savings generated from such projects. For example, officials at some installations said that they generally do not use installation-managed operation and maintenance funds for renewable energy projects because of competing demands for this funding for repairs and other maintenance of existing facilities on the installation. With regard to the Energy Conservation Investment Program, renewable energy projects must compete against other renewable energy projects as well as energy efficiency projects for limited funding and, according to officials, energy efficiency projects are often more cost-effective than renewable energy projects and receive higher priority for funding.

In addition to the benefits and drawbacks of the financing approaches, not all financing approaches are suitable in all circumstances. For example, an enhanced-use lease requires that a military department have land that is not needed for the time for public use, but is not excess to DOD's needs. In our previous report on enhanced-use leasing, we found cases where the military was leasing back property that had been included in an enhanced-use lease and cases where there appeared to be reasonable potential that the property included in a lease might be needed for military purposes over the lease's term, particularly in cases where the leased property was located in the interior, rather than at the perimeter, of the installation.[15] Additionally, although the military services could potentially use existing authorities to convey a renewable energy system to an electric utility company[16] or sell renewable energy to a utility,[17] the installation must have a renewable energy generation facility on the installation to use those authorities. According to military service headquarters officials, there are several issues with using these authorities for renewable energy projects; for example, officials said that the use of these authorities is complicated. Additionally, the military services may not have such facilities on the installations. Furthermore, some installations have not been able to use certain approaches because of constraints that are outside of the installation's control. For example, officials at three installations said that they are not able to use Utility Energy Service Contracts at their installations because the area electric utility company does not participate in the program. Additionally, officials at two installations said that they are limited in the alternative-financing approaches that they can use for renewable energy projects since the installations are serviced by regulated utilities. For example, officials at one of the installations said that they believe that they cannot implement any project in which they pay a contractor directly for the energy generated by the kilowatt hour—which is how contracts for projects financed through a power purchase agreement are typically paid—since the local utility is the only entity allowed to sell energy in the area.

DOD Plans to Expand Its Use of Alternative-Financing Approaches

Moving forward, DOD plans to expand its use of alternative-financing approaches for renewable energy projects. In its *Strategic Management Plan* for fiscal years 2012 and 2013, DOD established a goal to increase operational and installation energy efficiency to reduce costs and improve energy security, among other benefits.[18] One of the key initiatives within this goal is to expand the use of alternative financing for energy efficiency and renewable energy projects by 15 percent, as measured by the dollar

---

[15]GAO, *Defense Infrastructure: The Enhanced Use Lease Program Requires Management Attention*, GAO-11-574 (Washington, D.C.: June 30, 2011). The statutory provision requiring that the leased property not be needed for the time for public use was added in 2008, after many of the leases we reviewed in that report had been signed.

[16]10 U.S.C. § 2688.

[17]10 U.S.C. § 2916.

[18]Department of Defense, *Department of Defense Strategic Management Plan FY 2012-FY2013* (Sept. 20, 2011).

value of awarded contracts, by the end of fiscal year 2015. According to DOD's annual energy management report for fiscal year 2010, DOD awarded $323 million in contracts for energy efficiency and renewable energy projects that were financed with Energy Savings Performance Contracts and Utility Energy Service Contracts.[19] Thus, DOD would need to award nearly $50 million more in contracts, or a total of about $372 million, to meet this goal. An official from the Office of the Deputy Under Secretary of Defense (Installations and Environment) said that the Office of the Secretary of Defense plans to measure progress toward the goal annually based on the military services' submissions for DOD's Annual Energy Management Report. At the time of our review, the Office of the Secretary of Defense had not provided information to the military services about the goal, but an official said that the office is establishing a working group to assist the services in initiating and completing projects financed with alternative-financing approaches through improved collaboration and communication among stakeholders and sharing best practices.

Officials from two of the military services raised concerns about DOD's ability to meet the *Strategic Management Plan's* goal. One military service official said that the service has already planned enough projects funded with up-front appropriations to meet federal renewable energy goals for the next 2 years, making the number of alternatively financed projects within the service very low for fiscal year 2012 and unnecessary for fiscal year 2013. An official from another service indicated that DOD's ability to award more alternatively financed projects is outside of the military service's control and raised concerns that uncertainty about how the availability of federal and state incentives, as well as the condition of the financial markets, will affect that service's ability to attract private sector capital for alternatively financed projects. While officials from these two services raised concerns about meeting specific goals for awarding contracts for alternatively financed projects, officials from each of the military services' headquarters acknowledged that they expect that they will need to expand the use of alternative-financing approaches for renewable energy projects in the future to help the services meet the federal renewable energy goals in the long term.

---

[19]Department of Defense, *Department of Defense Annual Energy Management Report: Fiscal Year 2010* (July 2011).

Military Services Use Methods Designed to Ensure Good Value and Manage Risks, but Have Not Issued Comprehensive Guidance

Input from Headquarters Organizations and Supporting Agencies Is Designed to Ensure Good Value and Advantageous Contract Terms

According to a number of military service headquarters and installation officials, input from headquarters organizations and supporting agencies is a key method the military services use to help ensure that they receive good value and advantageous contract terms for renewable energy projects on installations. This input is designed to help ensure that the military services receive good value and advantageous contract terms for renewable energy projects since officials in the headquarters organizations and supporting agencies often have expertise and experience in overseeing the development and implementation of renewable energy projects and contracting for such projects. The military services differ in the organizations involved in developing and implementing renewable energy projects on installations, as well as the roles and responsibilities of these organizations. For each of the military services, installation officials generally develop smaller projects, such as projects to install solar panels on individual buildings or incorporate ground source heat pumps into individual buildings. The Army and Air Force have instituted more centralized processes—discussed below—to develop and implement larger renewable energy projects on installations, such as the large solar array project currently in development at Fort Irwin.

According to military service headquarters and installation officials, the military services' headquarters organizations and other supporting agencies provide input on proposed projects throughout the project development process, which the officials believe helps the military service obtain good value and advantageous contract terms for renewable energy projects on the installations. This input has taken different forms, as discussed below, and some formats for providing it were recently established and are still evolving.

- At the headquarters level, the Secretary of the Army established the Energy Initiatives Task Force in September 2011 to develop and implement large-scale renewable energy projects—defined as those greater than 10 megawatts—on Army installations. According to Army headquarters and installation officials, the task force provides knowledge and experience in developing large-scale projects and works with installation officials to develop and implement projects, including developing contracts. For example, the task force has worked with officials at Fort Bliss on three potential projects on the installation and with officials at Fort Irwin on a proposed 500-megawatt solar array. Additionally, the task force plans to provide information and assistance, as requested, to installations when developing and implementing smaller renewable energy projects. With regard to supporting agencies, the U.S. Army Corps of Engineers' Engineering and Support Center in Huntsville, Alabama, assists installations with developing and implementing renewable energy projects financed through Energy Savings Performance Contracts, Utility Energy Service Contracts, or the Energy Conservation Investment Program, including developing contracts for such projects. According to Army headquarters officials, the Engineering and Support Center's expertise in renewable energy technologies and contracting processes helps installations with the project development and contracting processes and to obtain good value and advantageous contract terms for renewable energy projects.
- At the headquarters level, the Navy developed an energy-return-on-investment tool to compare the financial and nonfinancial costs and benefits of renewable energy projects across the service. The tool, which was used for the first time for projects submitted as part of the fiscal year 2012 budget request, allows Navy headquarters officials to rank and compare energy projects submitted by installations and invest in projects that deliver the best return on investment. Navy headquarters officials review the proposed projects and, based on five criteria, make a recommendation to the installation about the best financing approach for the energy project. With regard to supporting agencies, the Naval Facilities Engineering Command's Engineering Service Center provides input on proposed projects by assisting installations with developing and implementing renewable energy projects, including developing contracts for projects. According to Navy headquarters and installation officials, the Engineering Service Center has expertise in renewable energy technologies, as well as contracting for a variety of types of projects, which helps in developing and implementing projects on the installations.
- Marine Corps headquarters officials consult with installations as needed to help installations develop and implement renewable energy

projects. According to a Marine Corps official, the Marine Corps has not established a formal or centralized process like the Navy and leaves decisions about financing approaches for renewable energy projects to installation commanders, who are responsible for developing renewable energy projects and identifying the financing approach. The official said this is due, in part, to the service's smaller size and more frequent contact between headquarters officials and installation energy managers that allow the headquarters officials to make suggestions informally to installations if headquarters officials think another financing approach is a better fit for a particular project. The Naval Facilities Engineering Command serves as the Marine Corps' contracting agent for construction projects and utility purchases, and the Marine Corps relies on its engineering expertise to identify measures to maximize the use of renewable energy sources within Marine Corps facilities, as well as in developing contracts for renewable energy projects.

- The Air Force Real Property Agency and the Air Force Civil Engineer Support Agency are beginning to work closely with Air Force installations to develop renewable energy projects, including selecting the financing approach for a project and developing the contract, according to Air Force Headquarters officials. The Air Force has begun to rely more on the Air Force Civil Engineer Support Agency to manage renewable energy projects funded with up-front appropriations or financed through power purchase agreements and—to the extent that they are used—Energy Savings Performance Contracts and Utility Energy Service Contracts, and on the Air Force Real Property Agency to manage all projects—including renewable energy projects—that use an enhanced-use lease. These agencies have each produced manuals that contain information on developing and implementing renewable energy projects financed through their respective approaches. Among other tasks, the Air Force Civil Engineer Support Agency reviewed the potential for large renewable energy projects at each Air Force Installation and is beginning to develop business case analyses for these projects, with a focus on completing the analyses for those projects that are most feasible first. According to Air Force headquarters and installation officials, the Air Force Civil Engineer Support Agency and Air Force Real Property Agency have expertise related to renewable energy and contracting processes that help ensure that the military service obtains good value and advantageous contract terms for renewable energy projects.

Cost Analyses Are Designed to Help Maximize Benefits and Mitigate Drawbacks or Risks of Financing Approaches, but Military Services Have Not Issued Comprehensive Guidance on Preparing Analyses

According to a number of military service headquarters and installation officials we interviewed, the military services use business case analyses or other more limited cost analyses, such as life-cycle cost analyses, as a second key method designed to help maximize the benefits and mitigate the drawbacks or risks of the selected financing approach; however, the military services have not issued comprehensive guidance on preparing such analyses for renewable energy projects. As we have previously reported, a business case analysis, sometimes called an economic analysis or cost-benefit analysis, is a comparative analysis that presents facts and supporting details among competing alternatives.[20] A business case analysis considers not only all of the life-cycle costs of a project, but also quantifiable and nonquantifiable benefits. It should be unbiased by considering various financing approaches and should not be developed solely for supporting a predetermined solution. Considering various financing approaches as part of the business case analysis can help maximize benefits and mitigate drawbacks of the selected financing approach if these benefits and drawbacks are included in the analysis.

Each of the military departments has issued guidance on business case analyses or economic analyses,[21] but a business case analysis is not mandatory for all renewable energy projects. Additionally, with the exception of the Navy guidance, which has an appendix on economic analyses for energy projects, the servicewide guidance is not specific to analyses for renewable energy projects. While the Navy guidance has an appendix on analyses for energy projects, it has not been updated since 1993 and does not provide information on the energy-return-on-investment tool, which—according to Navy headquarters officials—project officials are supposed to use when submitting renewable energy projects for review, nor does the guidance mention many of the available funding approaches for renewable energy projects, such as Energy Savings Performance Contracts or power purchase agreements. Moreover, while some installation officials we interviewed used their respective servicewide guidance, others said that they were not aware of the

---

[20]GAO, *GAO Cost Estimating and Assessment Guide: Best Practices for Developing and Managing Capital Program Costs*, GAO-09-3SP (Washington, D.C.: March 2009).

[21]Office of the Deputy Assistant Secretary of the Army (Cost and Economics), *U.S. Army Cost Benefit Analysis Guide* (Apr. 8, 2011); Naval Facilities Engineering Command, *Economic Analysis Handbook* (October 1993); Air Force Instruction 65-509, *Business Case Analysis* (Sept. 19, 2008) and Air Force Manual 65-510, *Business Case Analysis Procedures* (Sept. 22, 2008).

GAO-12-401 Renewable Energy Project Financing

guidance, and other officials who were aware of the guidance said that it is not used for analyses for most renewable energy projects. In addition to the servicewide guidance, the military services have limited information in their energy-related guidance on cost analyses for renewable energy projects. This information is often specific to the cost analyses for a particular financing approach, rather than applicable to all approaches.

Based on our review, the military services' energy-related guidance does not generally require a business case analysis, but typically requires that a lifecycle cost analysis should be completed for each renewable energy project. While these cost analyses may provide decisionmakers with information about the lifecycle costs of the project, they typically do not include an analysis of alternative methods for executing a given project. Additionally, we identified several renewable energy projects that were developed or implemented in recent years for which the project officials had not completed any cost analysis. As part of our review, we requested business case analyses or other supporting analyses, such as cost analyses, for 2 projects at each of the 10 installations included in our review, for a total of 20 projects. Based on our review of these analyses, we found that:

- Officials provided analyses for 14 of the 20 projects. Eight of these projects were placed in service between 2004 and 2011, and six projects were in development or under construction at the time of our review. Officials provided cost analyses in a variety of formats, from a real estate market study and best use analysis for a project financed through an enhanced-use lease to the form used by DOD to submit requirements and justification in support of requests for military construction to Congress, commonly referred to as a DD form 1391, for a project funded through the Energy Conservation Investment Program.
- Installation officials said that analyses were not conducted for 5 of the 20 projects. These five projects were placed in service from 2009 through 2011. According to installation officials, analyses were not performed for some of the projects because the renewable energy project was part of a larger project financed through an existing Energy Savings Performance Contract or was not part of the original military construction project. For example, an official at one installation said that an analysis was not performed for the renewable energy aspects included in a project to construct an operations facility paid for with military construction funds because project bids came in below estimates and the service's construction agent invested the difference in energy enhancements for the project. In another case, an

installation did not perform a cost analysis for a small project to install photovoltaic panels on the installation marquee because the photovoltaic panels had been purchased by another organization for another purpose and the command that oversees the installation was seeking proposals for using the panels.

- Installation officials could not locate the analysis that had been completed for the one remaining project, which was placed in service in 2009. An official said that the energy manager who developed the project has since left the position and that the project documentation at the installation did not include the cost analysis for the project.

In addition to our review of cost analyses, the DOD Inspector General and the Naval Audit Service have each conducted reviews of renewable energy projects funded with up-front appropriations from the American Recovery and Reinvestment Act. These auditors found that 13 Navy projects, 1 Marine Corps project, and 3 Air Force projects were not properly planned and supported, in that installation officials could not provide documentation to support payback analyses or did not perform cost analyses for some of the projects and, in other cases, implemented projects with limited financial benefits.[22] For example, the Naval Audit Service reported that the photovoltaic systems that they reviewed are expected to save about $704,000 annually after an investment of about $87 million; thus, it would take more than 120 years for the savings to exceed the costs.

Additionally, we identified nonquantifiable benefits that installation officials were unsure how to address or account for in a business case analysis or other cost analyses because the military services have not issued comprehensive guidance in these areas. One example is related to the consideration of energy security when developing business case analyses. DOD has emphasized the importance of renewable energy as a way to enhance energy security for installations. Recently, the Congress included a provision in the fiscal year 2012 National Defense

---

[22]Department of Defense Inspector General, *American Recovery and Reinvestment Act Wind Turbine Projects at Long-Range Radar Sites in Alaska Were Not Adequately Planned*, D-2011-116 (Arlington, Va., Sept. 30, 2011); *The Department of the Navy Spent Recovery Act Funds on Photovoltaic Projects That Were Not Cost-Effective*, D-2011-106 (Arlington, Va., Sept. 22, 2011); and *American Recovery and Reinvestment Act Project-Solar and Lighting at Naval Station Norfolk, Virginia*, D-2011-045 (Feb. 25, 2011). Naval Audit Service, *American Recovery and Reinvestment Act of 2009 – Photovoltaic Projects at Hampton Roads, VA, and Navy Installations in Florida, Texas, and Mississippi*, N2011-0060 (Washington, D.C.: Sept. 22, 2011).

Authorization Act related to considering the potential energy security benefits that a renewable energy project may provide to an installation.[23] However, officials at some installations and military service headquarters said that—with the exception of a Navy analytical tool—there is not a way to account for the potential energy security benefits that a project may provide to an installation in cost analyses.[24] Furthermore, some installation officials were unsure of how to account for the benefits of achieving service initiatives, such as the net zero initiative, in cost analyses. Without information on the costs and benefits to include in a cost analysis and how to account for nonquantifiable benefits, the military services cannot ensure that these analyses are comparable across renewable energy projects within a military service. Comparability of analyses across proposed projects within a service is important because results of the analysis are key factors used to prioritize renewable energy projects within the service for some financing approaches, such as the Energy Conservation Investment Program. Without processes and guidance to ensure that analyses are comparable across projects within the service, the military services cannot ensure that they are selecting and implementing the projects that best meet the goals of the financing approaches.

While installations provided cost analyses for 14 of the projects we reviewed, only 1 of the cost analyses we reviewed included an evaluation of different financing approaches. Specifically, the U.S. Air Force Academy developed a business case analysis for its photovoltaic solar array project that compared five options for financing the project, including one option in which a private developer would own the solar array and the installation would purchase energy through a power purchase agreement, and another alternative in which the installation would own the solar array.[25] We have previously reported in our work on

---

[23]Pub. Law No. 112-81 § 2822 (2011).

[24]Energy security is considered in the Navy's energy-return-on-investment tool in that the tool includes information on the project's ability to provide reliable energy to critical infrastructure in the project's overall score.

[25]The DOD Inspector General reviewed this project and found that the U.S. Air Force Academy incorrectly categorized all costs of the project as a utility company connection charge and incorrectly exempted the project from a subpart of the Federal Acquisition Regulation, but found that the Academy properly justified the project. Department of Defense Inspector General, *U.S. Air Force Academy Could Have Significantly Improved Planning, Funding, and Initial Execution of the American Recovery and Reinvestment Act Solar Project*, D-2011-071 (Arlington, Va., June 16, 2011).

capital planning that, as part of a review and approval process, leading organizations develop decision packages, such as business case analyses, to justify capital project requests.[26] We reported that leading practices include analyzing alternative approaches to address capital needs, which could help agencies determine whether alternative financing is the most appropriate way of acquiring capital. However, the cost analyses we reviewed do not include an analysis of the costs and benefits of different financing approaches because the military services have not issued comprehensive guidance for their renewable energy projects that require project officials to include such information. In 2011, the DOD Inspector General reported similar findings for two military services, stating that the Navy and Marine Corps energy policies did not include comprehensive processes for planning and selecting energy projects, to include requirements unique to energy projects.[27] As a result of not having comprehensive guidance to help ensure that installations complete the analyses and evaluate the costs and benefits of different financing approaches, the military services cannot ensure that decision makers will select the financing approach that best maximizes the benefits and mitigates the drawbacks or risks of the available financing approaches for renewable energy projects.

---

[26]GAO-05-55.

[27]Department of Defense Inspector General, *The Department of the Navy Spent Recovery Act Funds on Photovoltaic Projects That Were Not Cost-Effective*, D-2011-106 (Arlington, Va., Sept. 22, 2011). According to an official from the office of the DOD Inspector General, at the time of our review the Navy and Marine Corps had not yet implemented this recommendation.

Guidance, Training, and Other Resources Support Financing Decisions, but Inconsistencies in Interpreting Some Guidance and Ad Hoc Information Sharing among Project Officials May Limit the Use of Some Approaches

Amount of Guidance on Financing Approaches Has Increased, but Some Inconsistent Interpretations Exist

Within the past 3 years, the Under Secretary of Defense (Acquisition, Technology and Logistics); the Department of Energy; the military service headquarters or supporting agencies; and at least one installation have developed or updated guidance on the approaches that can be used to finance renewable energy projects on installations, but we found that different interpretations of some of this guidance affected the financing approaches each service used. At the department level, DOD's installation energy management instruction identifies partnerships with the private sector through alternative financing as a crucial tool for financing energy efficiency measures and allowing installations to improve their infrastructure, to include upgrades with renewable energy systems.[28] Additionally, the services have developed some guidance for their installations on alternative financing of renewable energy projects. For example, the Air Force Civil Engineer Support Agency and the Air Force Real Property Agency have developed detailed guidebooks to assist installations in developing power purchase agreements and enhanced-use leases, respectively, for renewable energy projects. The Army has developed an *Energy Savings Performance Contract Policy*

---

[28]Department of Defense Instruction 4170.11, *Installation Energy Management* (Dec. 11, 2009).

Handbook, and the Marine Corps has issued specific guidance to regional and installation commanders that they incorporate solar technologies for new facilities and major roof replacement projects when feasible.[29] The recent *Navy and Marine Corps Energy Project Management Guide* provides some guidance for selecting a financing approach for energy and water conservation projects in general. Navy officials said they saw the benefit of developing additional guidance on selecting the proper financing approach specifically for renewable projects, particularly in addressing factors such as renewable energy certificates and state incentives, among others. We also found an example of an installation that has established its own guidance. Fort Knox has developed a facility design guide that identifies energy design requirements to be included in contracts for energy projects at the installation to help it meet federal renewable energy goals.

DOD is taking steps to expand its guidance on financing approaches. DOD's installation energy management instruction briefly mentions the availability of two alternative-financing approaches—Utility Energy Service Contracts and Energy Savings Performance Contracts—but the instruction does not identify other approaches, nor does it provide guidance on selecting a financing approach. An official from the Office of the Deputy Under Secretary of Defense (Installations and Environment) told us that DOD is in the process of developing an overarching policy on the authorities available to fund renewable energy projects. The official expected the effort to result in a guidance memo and a handbook, although the office had not established time frames for completing these documents at the time of our review. Also, Army officials said they will be issuing new guidance to support the activities of the service's new Energy Initiatives Task Force. This guidance is projected to be published in spring 2012 and is expected to include a renewable energy execution plan and tool kits to provide a process for pursuing large-scale renewable energy projects.

Service and installation officials had varying perceptions of the availability, quality, and relevance of the guidance on financing renewable energy projects. Some officials believed existing guidance was adequate. Several officials acknowledged that more information on selecting the

---

[29]Assistant Deputy Commandant for Installations and Logistics (Facilities) Memorandum, *Roofing System Design and Construction for MILCON Building Projects and Major FSRM Roof Replacements* (Oct. 16, 2009).

financing approaches would be helpful, such as more information on regulatory issues or the best financing approach to use for renewable energy projects. In addition, some officials said that there was too much guidance available on developing renewable energy projects, noting that the amount of guidance was a challenge because available guidance is dispersed. Some officials said that it is left to installation-level officials to locate the information they need. Officials at one installation, for example, said that it would be useful to centralize the guidance on the different approaches available for funding renewable energy projects so that the information can be accessed in one location.

Despite the availability of this guidance on the various approaches that can be used to finance renewable energy projects, we found instances where different interpretations of some of this guidance affected the financing approaches the services used because DOD has not issued overarching guidance on the selection and use of these financing approaches. For example, Army and Navy installations use Energy Savings Performance Contracts and Utility Energy Service Contracts for their renewable energy projects, often citing the benefits of having a developer construct and manage the project and having established relationships with local utility companies. The Air Force, on the other hand, has used Energy Savings Performance Contracts and Utility Energy Service Contracts in the past, but Air Force Facilities Energy Center officials told us they are not currently using them to finance new renewable energy projects because of uncertainty about whether such projects are considered energy conservation measures and whether the projects are economically viable. Air Force officials told us that projects with long payback periods are typically not economically viable and additional costs, such as financing costs and other overhead costs to manage contracts, and the ability to sell renewable energy certificates or have access to state tax incentives can affect whether an Energy Savings Performance Contract or Utility Energy Service Contract is the most cost effective approach to finance a renewable energy project.[30] Developers can sometimes use the revenues from the sale of renewable energy certificates or tax incentives that some states make available to commercial entities or utilities, such as sales tax exemptions or rebates

---

[30]In the United States, renewable energy production essentially creates two products: the energy itself and an associated commodity, called a renewable energy certificate, which represents a certain amount of energy generated using a renewable resource. Renewable energy certificates are bought and sold in a fashion similar to stocks and bonds.

for implementing certain renewable technologies, for example, to help offset the higher costs of renewable energy projects.

As a result of these different concerns and interpretations, the military services may not be taking full advantage of the various financing approaches that are available to finance projects to meet renewable energy goals. For example, officials from both the Office of the Deputy Under Secretary of Defense (Installations and Environment) and the Department of Energy described how different interpretations among the military services regarding one authority for power purchase agreements previously limited the use of that authority.[31] Until recently, some services interpreted this authority as applying to geothermal energy only. DOD has since clarified this authority as applying to all renewable energy sources and the services are beginning to implement more projects using this authority, such as a project to increase production at a developer-operated power plant that is powered by methane gas from the landfill adjacent to Marine Corps Air Station Miramar.

Training on Financing Approaches Is Available within and outside DOD

DOD personnel participated in training provided by DOD and other sources on the various financing approaches for renewable energy projects and were generally satisfied with this training. Within DOD, the services provide training to installation personnel on developing renewable energy projects, including on how to select a financing approach. Much of the service-level training is provided by the services' commands or agencies responsible for engineering or installation management. For example, the Air Force Civil Engineer Support Agency developed just-in-time training that provides basic information about power purchase agreements and identifies the steps to follow in pursuing projects financed with this approach. According to Air Force officials, the agency also meets with representatives from the service's 13 major commands as part of the agency's regular program management reviews to educate the commands on various aspects of renewable energy, including the financing approaches for renewable energy projects. The Army Corps of Engineers has a training program for personnel involved in contracting for Energy Savings Performance Contracts and Utility Energy Service Contracts, and the Energy Initiatives Task Force plans to implement a training curriculum on developing large-scale renewable

---

[31]10 U.S.C. § 2922a.

energy projects using alternative financing, within the next 12 months. Additionally, Army Installation Management Command provides training to installation energy managers. Some service officials also told us that their energy management personnel can receive training through courses provided by military educational institutions, such as the Air Force Institute of Technology.

Personnel at the military service headquarters and installations also receive training from other sources, particularly through the Department of Energy's Federal Energy Management Program's online and on-site training. Department of Energy officials told us that the Federal Energy Management Program provides monthly training opportunities on a variety of issues, including alternative-financing approaches, through its seminars and other training courses, which are offered via Webcast and interactive television. Additionally, the Federal Energy Management Program provides on-site training to agencies upon request. Department of Energy officials told us that although the Federal Energy Management Program has not tailored its existing workshop and Webcast training specifically for DOD, presenters generally provide information on DOD's unique authorities for renewable energy projects.[32] Other training venues include sessions held in conjunction with conferences and courses provided by industry and local institutions of higher education. Officials at Marine Corps Air Station Miramar, for example, told us they can receive energy-related training from the local utility as well as from a local nonprofit organization and an area university.

Officials were generally satisfied with the availability, quality, and relevance of the training they received from DOD and other sources, although some officials at the military service headquarters and installations acknowledged gaps in the training and the need to continue to update the training as new guidance is issued. As with guidance, some officials told us they were interested in receiving additional training in areas such as federal and state incentives that are available for use on renewable energy projects or state and jurisdictional variables that can affect an installation's ability to implement such projects. Additionally, some installation officials cited concerns with having sufficient staff

---

[32]Department of Energy officials explained that they typically tailor their on-site training to the needs of the individual agency or site.

available to put that training to use in developing and managing renewable energy projects.

Other Resources Provide Information-Sharing Opportunities, but Coordination among Project Officials Is Ad Hoc and Not Formalized

In addition to training opportunities, DOD and other agencies have made available other resources—such as conferences, working groups, and consultations with energy experts—to assist officials in selecting financing approaches for renewable energy projects, but coordination at the installation level remains ad hoc and not formalized. First, DOD officials participate in numerous energy-related conferences, such as the annual GovEnergy conference that provides energy management training and information to federal employees and government stakeholders. In addition to this training, GovEnergy also provides opportunities for participants to share information, both formally and informally, about best practices and the lessons that they have learned from their experiences developing and implementing renewable energy projects; develop partnerships with energy managers from other federal agencies; and attend meetings specific to their service that are held in conjunction with the conference. Military service officials also attend energy forums, such as the Naval Energy Forum or the Army and Air Force Energy Forum. These forums are a venue for the services to get the perspectives of senior leadership from DOD, federal agencies, Congress, and industry regarding energy, including sharing information on their experiences developing and implementing renewable energy projects. Second, military service headquarters officials told us that the service headquarters' energy focal points meet regularly to share information on energy issues, including financing approaches. Third, headquarters and subordinate command level officials participate in a variety of federal working groups, such as the Federal Utility Partnership Working Group, the Energy Savings Performance Contract Steering Committee, and others. The Federal Utility Partnership Working Group consists of federal agencies, utilities, and energy service organizations and meets twice per year to, among other things, develop strategies and procedures for the implementation of renewable energy projects at federal sites. Finally, Department of Energy officials told us that, in addition to one-on-one consultations with Federal Energy Management Program experts, installations can also work through the Federal Energy Management Program for access to experts at the Department of Energy laboratories. For example, the Pacific Northwest National Laboratory issued several reports assessing various military installations for potential renewable energy project opportunities, many for projects funded through the American Recovery and Reinvestment Act of 2009. The Department of Energy also publishes case studies and articles related to renewable energy project financing on its Web site and collects and disseminates information on other resources through interagency meetings and contacts with agency representatives.

In addition to these federal-level efforts, we found that each service has developed mechanisms for sharing information within the service, such as best practices and lessons that officials learned from the projects, including working groups, Web sites, and service-specific conferences. The Navy, for example, has established an Energy Project Execution Team comprised of Naval Facilities Engineering Command engineers that meets several times a year to share information about projects and best practices or lessons learned from implementing all types of energy projects. Examples of Army Web sites used to share best practices include the Installation Management Command's Garrison Commanders' Web site and the Assistant Chief of Staff for Installation Management's energy program Web site, which Army officials described as sources for learning about renewable energy projects at other Army installations. Similarly, both Air Combat Command and the Air Force Civil Engineer Support Agency have communities of practice that maintain Web sites with information such as guidance and policy documents related to energy, examples of projects, and sample military construction project data sheets for installations to download. The military services also sponsor conferences, such as the Army's January 2012 net zero conference that was intended to support the efforts of the Army's overall net zero initiative and pilot installations through training sessions, information from industry representatives, and interactions among Army installations as they move toward the net zero goals in energy, water, and waste.

Additionally, we found some coordination among the services within geographical regions. For example, Fort Irwin officials highlighted the coordination that takes place through the Desert Managers Group. This group was established in 1997 under the Mojave Desert Ecosystem Program to address environmental and energy issues in the region and includes stakeholders from other federal agencies; local utilities, governments, and institutions of higher education; non-governmental organizations; and the other installations in the region—Edwards Air Force Base, Marine Corps Air Ground Combat Center Twentynine Palms, and Naval Air Weapons Station China Lake. According to the officials, the four DOD bases hold a separate session in conjunction with this group's quarterly meetings to share ideas and their experiences, to include exchanging information on energy issues. Similarly, officials at Fort Bliss told us that they have begun discussions to improve collaboration with two New Mexico installations located nearby—Holloman Air Force Base and the Army's White Sands Missile Range—to assess the potential for regional energy solutions.

While information sharing is taking place across the services at the headquarters level, opportunities to share information across the services are limited at the installation level even though some decisions about the renewable energy projects are made at the installation level. According to the *Standards for Internal Control in the Federal Government*, information should be communicated to the management and others within an organization who need it and in a form and within a time frame that enables them to carry out their responsibilities.[33] These standards state, among other things, that effective communications should occur in a broad sense with information flowing down, across, and up the organization and that there should exist adequate means of communicating with and obtaining information from external stakeholders that may have a significant impact on the agency's achieving its goals. However, DOD has not instituted a formalized process to share information on the financing of renewable energy projects across the military services at the installation level. Officials we spoke with at several installations said that coordination and information sharing at their level was done on an ad hoc basis and told us that they would benefit from more formalized coordination and access to information among installations from the different services on best practices regarding renewable energy projects. For example, some officials said that they learned about other services' renewable energy projects through participating in conferences but said they would benefit from a more formalized way to learn about how other services are selecting and implementing renewable energy projects. Because the coordination and communication process remains ad hoc and not formalized, DOD cannot ensure that officials responsible for selecting a financing approach have timely access on an ongoing basis to information on the approaches that their counterparts from other services have used, including best practices and the lessons that other officials have learned from their experiences, which could better assist them in selecting a financing approach that maximizes the benefits and minimizes the drawbacks or risks of that approach.

---

[33]GAO, *Standards for Internal Control in the Federal Government*, GAO/AIMD-00-21.3.1 (Washington, D.C.: November 1999).

Conclusions

DOD spends billions of dollars each year to provide electricity and other energy to more than 500 permanent installations worldwide and has been developing renewable energy projects to help reduce these costs, meet federal renewable energy goals, and improve energy security on its installations. DOD is planning to increase its use of renewable energy at installations to meet federal renewable energy goals, as well as service-specific goals, in the coming years and plans to continue financing these efforts through both up-front appropriations and alternative financing. However, without processes and comprehensive guidance in place to ensure that project officials complete the analyses and evaluate the costs and benefits of different financing approaches, the military services cannot ensure that decision makers—whether they are at the installation level or headquarters level—are choosing the financing approach that best maximizes the benefits and mitigates the drawbacks of the available financing approaches. Additionally, while some decisions are becoming more centralized within the military services, installation officials still play a key role in developing and implementing renewable energy projects on installations. DOD, the military services, and subordinate organizations are developing additional guidance to assist officials in making decisions about the financing approach for a particular project; however, without overarching guidance to establish a clear and consistent framework for using the alternative-financing approaches, military services and installations may not have all of the information that they need to take full advantage of all available financing approaches. Similarly, the military services have established processes to share information and best practices or lessons learned on financing approaches for renewable energy projects at the headquarters level, as well as within each military service, but without such information at the installation level, where the project proponents are usually located, DOD may be missing opportunities to implement projects using different financing approaches that could help the department meet its renewable energy goals in a cost effective way.

Recommendations for Executive Action

GAO is making three recommendations to the Secretary of Defense.

- To better ensure that the military services select a financing approach that best maximizes the benefits and mitigates the drawbacks or risks of available approaches, we recommend that the Secretary of Defense direct the Under Secretary of Defense (Acquisition, Technology and Logistics), the Deputy Under Secretary of Defense (Installations and Environment), and the military services to issue comprehensive guidance that establishes and clearly describes the military services' processes to ensure that business case analyses are completed and that these analyses fully consider the costs and benefits of different financing approaches for renewable energy projects.

- To help enable officials to better understand how to use all of the approaches that are available to finance projects to meet renewable energy goals, we recommend that the Secretary of Defense direct the Under Secretary of Defense (Acquisition, Technology and Logistics) and the Deputy Under Secretary of Defense (Installations and Environment) to develop overarching guidance about the use of available financing approaches for financing renewable energy projects and direct the military services to update their guidance accordingly. At a minimum, this guidance should include the requirements and restrictions of the underlying authorities and any DOD-specific guidelines for using up-front appropriations and alternative-financing approaches for renewable energy projects.

- To improve the information-sharing resources that are available to assist officials in selecting a financing approach that maximizes the benefits and minimizes the drawbacks or risks of that approach, we recommend that the Secretary of Defense direct the Under Secretary of Defense (Acquisition, Technology and Logistics) and the Deputy Under Secretary of Defense (Installations and Environment) to develop a formalized communications process, such as a shared Web site or other appropriate approach, that will enable officials at military installations to have timely access on an ongoing basis to information related to financing renewable energy projects on other installations, including best practices and lessons that other installations have learned from their experiences in financing their renewable energy projects.

Agency Comments and Our Evaluation

In written comments on a draft of this report, DOD partially concurred with one recommendation and fully concurred with two others. DOD's comments are reprinted in their entirety in appendix IV. DOD also provided technical comments, which we have incorporated as appropriate. The Department of Energy also reviewed a draft of this report but did not provide any comments.

DOD partially concurred with our first recommendation to issue comprehensive guidance related to preparing business case analyses for renewable energy projects. DOD stated that the department recognizes the importance of establishing credible and effective guidance for such analyses, but does not believe that a business case analysis must include an analysis of all potential financing approaches because some approaches would not apply to some projects. Nothing in our recommendation prevents DOD from exercising judgment in which financing approaches are or are not considered as appropriate. As stated in our report, we agree that not all financing approaches are suitable in all circumstances. As such, we would not expect a business case analysis to consider the costs and benefits of financing approaches that were not suitable for a specific project. For example, we would not expect a military service to analyze the costs and benefits of a project financed through an enhanced-use lease if the installation did not have adequate land available for the purpose in the first place. However, we believe that in most circumstances more than one financing approach may be suitable for a project and, therefore, should be considered as part of the business case analysis. We believe that DOD's comments are consistent with the intent of our recommendation.

DOD concurred with our second recommendation to develop overarching guidance about the use of available financing approaches and direct the military services to update their guidance accordingly. DOD expects to develop this guidance, which will include requirements and restrictions related to the authorities and discuss the variety of approaches and strategies for financing renewable energy projects although the department did not specify a time frame for taking this action.

DOD concurred with our third recommendation to develop a formalized communications process to share information on financing renewable energy projects among installations. DOD stated that the department agrees that it is necessary to develop such a process, which will enhance DOD's ability to leverage best practices among installations and personnel. DOD plans to initiate an alternative-financing energy working group with representatives from around the department for this purpose. As long as this working group establishes some method to allow project-level officials to share information, including best practices and lessons learned from their experiences, we believe this planned action meets the intent of our recommendation.

We are sending copies of this report to the Secretary of Defense; the Secretaries of the Army, the Navy, and the Air Force; the Commandant of the Marine Corps; the Secretary of Energy; the Director, Office of Management and Budget; and interested congressional committees. In addition, this report is available at no charge on the GAO Web site at http://www.gao.gov/

If you or your staff have any questions about this report, please contact Brian J. Lepore at (202) 512-4523 or leporeb@gao.gov or Frank Rusco at (202) 512-3841 or ruscof@gao.gov. Contact points for our Offices of Congressional Relations and Public Affairs may be found on the last page of this report. GAO staff who made key contributions to this report are listed in appendix V.

Brian J. Lepore
Director
Defense Capabilities and Management

Frank Rusco
Director
Natural Resources and Environment

List of Committees

The Honorable Carl Levin
Chairman
The Honorable John McCain
Ranking Member
Committee on Armed Services
United States Senate

The Honorable Daniel K. Inouye
Chairman
The Honorable Thad Cochran
Ranking Member
Subcommittee on Defense
Committee on Appropriations
United States Senate

The Honorable Howard P. McKeon
Chairman
The Honorable Adam Smith
Ranking Member
Committee on Armed Services
House of Representatives

The Honorable C. W. Bill Young
Chairman
The Honorable Norman D. Dicks
Ranking Member
Subcommittee on Defense
Committee on Appropriations
House of Representatives

Appendix I: Scope and Methodology

This appendix provides information on the scope of our work and methodology to (1) determine the approaches that the military services are using to finance renewable energy projects on military installations and the factors that the services consider in selecting a financing approach, (2) assess the extent to which the military services have established methods to obtain good value and advantageous contract terms for renewable energy projects on installations and maximize benefits and mitigate drawbacks or risks of financing approaches, and (3) identify the extent to which the military services have developed guidance, training, and other resources to assist officials in selecting and implementing financing approaches for renewable energy projects. For the purposes of this review, we defined "renewable energy" as energy derived from any of the following fuel sources: biomass; geothermal; hydropower; solar; wind; ocean energy, including wave, tidal, current, and ocean thermal energy; and other sources, such as landfill gas and municipal solid waste, that are constantly replenished. This energy can be applied in any form, including electricity, heating, or small-scale applications such as streetlights or trash compactors. Our definition differs from the definitions used for computation of the relevant federal energy goals, as noted in the body of the report. We focused on facilities energy efforts in the United States and overseas and excluded operational energy and vehicles from our review. Additionally, we focused on the military services' renewable energy efforts—which comprise the vast majority of DOD's renewable energy projects—and excluded the defense agencies and other defense organizations from our review since their projects represent a small subset of the total. Finally, we focused on DOD's efforts to generate renewable energy and excluded from our review nuclear energy and efforts that only addressed energy efficiency or conservation.

To determine the extent to which the military services are using available approaches to finance renewable energy projects on military installations, we first reviewed applicable legal authorities, DOD and Department of Energy guidance and training materials, and reports by GAO and other federal agencies to identify available financing approaches. We also discussed the available funding approaches with knowledgeable officials from the DOD and Department of Energy offices mentioned below. Then we compared the financing approaches that DOD has used to the available approaches. We obtained information on the military services' renewable energy projects that were designed, constructed, or operating in fiscal year 2010 from the inventory generated during another GAO review.[1] We compared the list to service-specific and DOD-wide sources of information to identify additional projects that were in design, under construction, or began operating in fiscal year 2011 that were not included in the original list, as well as to identify the approach used to finance the renewable energy project, so that our final list included all projects that were in design, under construction, or currently operating in fiscal year 2011. We provided the updated lists to the military services and requested that service officials (1) review the data to ensure that the information was accurate, (2) provide updates to the data, including any additional projects not identified in the list provided, to include any new projects in fiscal year 2011, and (3) provide information that we were unable to obtain from another source, such as information on the financing approach. We used this data collection and verification process to assess the reliability of the data and we found the data to be sufficiently reliable for the purposes of this report.

Additionally, to determine the factors that the military services consider when selecting a financing approach for renewable energy projects, to include the benefits and drawbacks or risks of each of the financing approaches, we interviewed officials from the Office of the Deputy Under Secretary of Defense (Installations and Environment); the Defense Logistics Agency-Energy office; each of the military service headquarters and their supporting agencies, including the U.S. Army Corps of Engineers Engineering and Support Center (Huntsville), the Naval Facilities Engineering Command, the Air Force Civil Engineer Support Agency, and the Air Force Real Property Agency; 10 selected installations; and the Department of Energy. To identify the installations to include in our review, we first selected a nonprobability sample of eight installations—two installations per service—to get a mix of the types of financing approaches used, the types of renewable energy projects implemented, and geographic diversity, with an emphasis on installations that have used multiple financing sources and implemented different types of projects on an individual installation. These eight installations are Fort Irwin and Marine Corps Air Station Miramar, California; the U.S. Air Force Academy, Colorado; Naval Air Station Jacksonville, Florida; Fort Knox, Kentucky; Marine Corps Air Station Beaufort, South Carolina; Hill

---

[1]GAO, *Renewable Energy: Federal Agencies Implement Hundreds of Initiatives*, GAO-12-260 (Washington, D.C.: Feb. 27, 2012). See appendix I for information on data collection for the original list.

Air Force Base, Utah; and Naval Air Station Oceana, Virginia. We then selected two additional installations with unique characteristics to include in our sample: Nellis Air Force Base, Nevada, is the home to one of the largest solar photovoltaic arrays in the nation and Fort Bliss, Texas, is planned to be one of the Army's two "integrated net zero" installations.[2]

To determine the extent to which the military services have established methods to maximize benefits and mitigate risks of financing approaches and obtain good value and advantageous contract terms for renewable energy projects on military installations, we reviewed guidance, directives, and instructions from DOD and the military services related to renewable energy projects. We also reviewed related guidance from the Office of Management and Budget for cost effectiveness analyses. Additionally, we reviewed project documentation for selected projects at the 10 installations included in our scope. For example, we requested business case analyses or similar analyses for 2 projects at each of the 10 selected installations and reviewed these analyses. We also interviewed officials at the Office of the Deputy Under Secretary of Defense (Installations and Environment), the military service headquarters and their supporting agencies, and the 10 selected installations. Additionally, we reviewed previous GAO reports related to the identified methods to better understand the methods.

To determine the extent to which DOD has developed guidance, training, and other resources to assist officials in selecting and implementing the financing approaches for renewable energy projects, we reviewed existing guidance developed by the Under Secretary of Defense (Acquisition, Technology and Logistics) and the military services. We also reviewed information on the training offered through DOD, the Department of Energy, and other sources, such as conferences. Additionally, we spoke with officials at the Office of the Deputy Under Secretary of Defense (Installations and Environment), the Defense Logistics Agency-Energy office, the military service headquarters and supporting agencies, and the 10 selected installations to obtain their

---

[2]Integrated net zero installations are comprised of three components: net zero energy, net zero water, and net zero waste. A net zero energy installation produces as much energy on site as it consumes in a year. A net zero water installation limits the consumption of freshwater resources and returns water back to the same watershed so as not to deplete the groundwater and surface water resources of that region in quantity and quality over the course of a year. A net zero waste installation reduces, reuses, and recovers waste streams, converting them to resource values with zero landfill over the course of a year.

perspectives on the availability, quality, and relevance of the guidance, training, and other resources. We also spoke with officials from the Department of Energy's Federal Energy Management Program to discuss the types and quantity of training their agency provides to DOD personnel.

We conducted this performance audit from June 2011 through April 2012 in accordance with generally accepted government auditing standards. Those standards require that we plan and perform the audit to obtain sufficient, appropriate evidence to provide a reasonable basis for our findings and conclusions based on our audit objectives. We believe that the evidence obtained provides a reasonable basis for our findings and conclusions based on our audit objectives.

Appendix II: Selected Financing Approaches Available for Acquisition of Renewable Energy or Development of Renewable Energy Projects on DOD Installations

Financing approach	Summary of approach related to financing renewable energy projects	Selected legal authorities for approach[a]
Up-front appropriations		
Annual military construction appropriations, including the Energy Conservation Investment Program (ECIP)	The acquisition, construction, installation, and equipment of temporary or permanent public works, installations, facilities, and real property is typically financed through military construction appropriations. The Energy Conservation Investment Program is a subset of the defensewide Military Construction program specifically designated for projects that save energy or reduce defense energy costs. The program supports construction of new high-efficiency energy systems and the improvement and modernization of existing systems. Projects funded through the Energy Conservation Investment Program can include energy efficiency, water conservation, and renewable energy projects.	10 U.S.C. § 2802, et seq. See also annual military construction appropriation acts, e.g. the Military Construction and Veterans Affairs and Related Agencies Appropriations Act, 2010, Pub. L. No. 111-117, Division E (2009)
Operation and maintenance appropriations	Certain small military construction projects may be undertaken with operation and maintenance funds (limited to projects costing less than $750,000), and these projects could include renewable energy projects. Additionally, certain repairs or renovations to existing structures may also be financed through operation and maintenance funds. These renovations may sometimes include energy efficiencies or other energy-related repairs.	10 U.S.C. § 2805 10 U.S.C. § 2854 10 U.S.C. § 2811
Other up-front appropriations	Periodically, Congress makes available other direct appropriations that can be used for renewable energy projects. For example, DOD used funds from the American Recovery and Reinvestment Act of 2009 on renewable energy projects. DOD has also used appropriated funds programmed for the Environmental Security Technology Certification Program, DOD's environmental technology demonstration and validation program, to fund renewable energy projects on DOD installations.	See, for example, military construction funds provided in the American Recovery and Reinvestment Act of 2009 (Pub. L. No. 111-5 (2009)).

Appendix II: Selected Financing Approaches
Available for Acquisition of Renewable Energy
or Development of Renewable Energy Projects
on DOD Installations

Financing approach	Summary of approach related to financing renewable energy projects	Selected legal authorities for approach[a]
Alternative financing		
Energy Savings Performance Contract (ESPC)	An Energy Savings Performance Contract is a contract between a federal agency and an energy service company. The energy service company conducts a comprehensive energy audit for the federal facility and identifies improvements to save energy. In consultation with the federal agency, the energy service company designs and constructs a project that meets the agency's needs and arranges the necessary financing. The contractor guarantees that the improvements will generate energy cost savings sufficient to pay for the project over the term of the contract. Payment to the contractor is contingent upon realizing a guaranteed stream of future energy and cost savings, with any savings in excess of that guaranteed by the contractor accruing to the federal government. Contract terms for Energy Savings Performance Contracts can extend up to 25 years.	42 U.S.C. § 8287
Utility Energy Service Contract (UESC)	In a Utility Energy Service Contract, a utility arranges financing to cover the capital costs of a project, which are repaid by the agency over the contract term, usually based on estimated cost savings generated by the energy efficiency measures. One key difference between a Utility Energy Service Contract and an Energy Savings Performance Contract is that Utility Energy Service Contract contractors are not necessarily required to guarantee that the project will generate sufficient savings to repay the capital costs.	10 U.S.C. § 2913 42 U.S.C. § 8256

**Appendix II: Selected Financing Approaches
Available for Acquisition of Renewable Energy
or Development of Renewable Energy Projects
on DOD Installations**

Financing approach	Summary of approach related to financing renewable energy projects	Selected legal authorities for approach[a]
Power purchase agreement (PPA)	Power purchase agreements for renewable energy may take several forms, but all are essentially agreements to purchase renewable energy from a private sector energy producer. In some cases a power purchase agreement may simply be a long-term purchase agreement entered into with a utility to lock in an attractive rate for renewable energy. Another potential use of power purchase agreements is in conjunction with enhanced-use leasing as an incentive for the private lessee. In this scenario, a private entity would finance the construction of power generation equipment and installation on government land and provide for operation and maintenance of the system for the term of the contract. The system would typically be privately owned and the federal facility would agree to purchase the electricity through a long-term power purchase agreement. DOD refers to power purchase agreements undertaken using certain authorities as "energy services contracts." The length of the allowed contract term varies based on the authority used for the power purchase agreement. Under 10 U.S.C. § 2410q, DOD can enter into contracts for up to 5 years generally, or up to 10 years in certain circumstances. Under 10 U.S.C. § 2922a, DOD can enter into contracts for up to 30 years. Under 10 U.S.C. § 2809, DOD can enter into contracts for up to 32 years, excluding the period for construction.	10 U.S.C. § 2410q 10 U.S.C. § 2922a 10 U.S.C. § 2809
Enhanced-use lease (EUL)[b]	An enhanced-use lease is a lease that allows the military services to outlease available nonexcess real property that is not needed for the time for government use to the private sector in return for cash or in-kind consideration. Enhanced-use leases have been used for a wide range of facility improvement projects, renovations, repair, or new acquisitions, to include renewable energy projects. The length of a contract for an enhanced-use lease is subject to certain conditions, but there is no firm time limit. We have previously reported that these leases are often entered into for long periods, such as 25- or 50-year terms.	10 U.S.C. § 2667

Appendix II: Selected Financing Approaches
Available for Acquisition of Renewable Energy
or Development of Renewable Energy Projects
on DOD Installations

Financing approach	Summary of approach related to financing renewable energy projects	Selected legal authorities for approach[a]
Convey utility system to a utility company	In this approach the secretary of a military department may convey existing utility systems owned by DOD to a utility company in exchange for compensation. One type of contemplated compensation is provision of power at reduced rates. Contract terms are limited to 10 years or, subject to certain conditions, up to 50 years.	10 U.S.C. § 2688
Sell electricity to a utility	This approach involves the secretary of a military department selling certain kinds of electricity generated on a military installation to a utility (subject to certain requirements) and depositing the proceeds in the appropriation account available to the relevant military department for the supply of electrical energy. Those funds may be used (under certain conditions) to finance certain energy-related military construction projects.	10 U.S.C. § 2916
Lease-to-own energy production facilities	This approach involves the secretary of a military department entering into an agreement with a private sector entity to "lease to own" certain facilities provided at the expense of the contractor on a military installation. At the end of the lease, title to the property would vest in the United States. This approach can be used for a variety of facilities, including energy production facilities. Contract terms may not exceed 32 years.	10 U.S.C. § 2812

Source: GAO analysis of approaches and legal authorities.

Note: We did not include in our analysis certain other approaches that could potentially be available to DOD for the financing of renewable energy projects, such as approaches that could only be employed in narrowly defined situations or that may not be useful departmentwide. For example we excluded 10 U.S.C. § 2686, which authorizes the secretary of a military department to sell or contract to sell certain specific utilities (including electrical power) to purchasers in the immediate vicinity of an activity of the relevant service under certain unusual circumstances (e.g., the utility is not otherwise available from a local source).

[a]Many of these approaches may be authorized by several legal authorities used in concert, or independently authorized by multiple legal authorities. Our table includes a selection of authorities relevant to each approach, but is not necessarily exhaustive.

[b]The military services refer to certain leases of real property undertaken pursuant to the authority in 10 U.S.C. § 2667 as "enhanced-use leases."

Appendix III: Summary of Benefits and Drawbacks of Selected Financing Approaches for Renewable Energy Projects

Figure 1: Summary of Benefits of Selected Financing Approaches for Renewable Energy Projects Identified by Interviewed Officials at Military Service Headquarters and Selected Installations

Benefits	Annual military construction appropriations[a]	Energy Conservation Investment Program[a]	Operation and maintenance appropriations	Energy Savings Performance Contract	Utility Energy Service Contract	Power purchase agreement	Enhanced-use lease
	Up-front appropriations			Alternative financing approaches			
Contractor may be eligible for certain incentives that can help make a project more cost-effective				✓		✓	
Limited or no agency up-front capital is required, can finance project over time while getting benefit of the project immediately				✓	✓	✓	✓
Developer operates and maintains equipment or operations and maintenance can be added to contract				✓	✓	✓	✓
Known long-term electricity price allows service to better budget for energy costs						✓	
Contractor guarantees energy savings				✓			
No additional private sector financing charges makes project cheaper for the government in the long term	✓	✓	✓				
Installation or military service receives full savings from implementing the project immediately rather than after financing is repaid	✓	✓	✓				
Funding is specifically for energy projects, so less competition than for other sources		✓					
Limited paperwork requirements to request funding		✓	✓				
Generally the contract is for purchasing energy, so the government does not have to pay the contractor if the project does not produce energy, depending on the terms of the contract.						✓	✓
Contract is with the local utility, with which the installation already has an established relationship					✓		

Source: GAO analysis of interviews with DOD officials.

[a]For the purposes of our analysis, we considered benefits specifically mentioned for the Energy Conservation Investment Program separate from the benefits of annual military construction appropriations.

Figure 2: Summary of Drawbacks or Risks of Selected Financing Approaches for Renewable Energy Projects Identified by Interviewed Officials at Military Service Headquarters and Selected Installations

Drawbacks or risks	Up-front appropriations			Alternative financing approaches			
	Annual military construction appropriations[a]	Energy Conservation Investment Program[a]	Operation and maintenance appropriations[a]	Energy Savings Performance Contract	Utility Energy Service Contract	Power purchase agreement	Enhanced-use lease
Projects are generally more costly to the government due to private financing costs				✓	✓	✓	✓
Limited federal sector experience in implementing the approach; installation officials may not be familiar with approach						✓	
Approach may not be available for all facilities or installations				✓	✓		✓
Cannot ordinarily leverage state tax incentives because project is owned by the federal government	✓	✓	✓	✓			
Some key incentives that make projects financially viable are ending soon or public funding for such incentives is limited				✓		✓	✓
Installation is responsible for operation and maintenance of equipment, but personnel may not have needed expertise	✓	✓	✓				
Lengthy process to receive project approval and funding	✓	✓	✓				
Contracts are often complex, challenging, or time consuming to develop and implement				✓		✓	✓
Concerns with, or difficulties in, using approach specifically for renewable energy				✓	✓	✓	✓
Projects require extensive or time-consuming analysis to develop		✓				✓	✓
Limited funding available and projects must compete for funding	✓	✓	✓				
Limits on total cost of project established in law, so approach can only be used to fund small projects that do not generate much renewable energy			✓				
Installation or military service does not receive full amount of savings from the project until the contractor is repaid				✓	✓		
Termination of contract may require payment to the contractor				✓	✓	✓	✓

Source: GAO analysis of interviews with DOD officials.

[a]For the purposes of our analysis, we considered drawbacks or risks specifically mentioned for the Energy Conservation Investment Program separate from the drawbacks or risks of annual military construction appropriations.

GAO-12-401 Renewable Energy Project Financing

Appendix IV: Comments from the Department of Defense

OFFICE OF THE UNDER SECRETARY OF DEFENSE
3000 DEFENSE PENTAGON
WASHINGTON, DC 20301-3000

ACQUISITION,
TECHNOLOGY
AND LOGISTICS

MAR 2 3 2012

Mr. Brian J. Lepore
Director, Defense Capabilities and Management
U.S. Government Accountability Office
441 G Street, N.W.
Washington, DC 20548

Dear Mr. Lepore:

This is the Department of Defense (DoD) response to the GAO draft report, GAO-12-401, "RENEWABLE ENERGY PROJECT FINANCING: Improved Guidance and Information Sharing Needed for DOD Project-Level Officials," dated April 2012 (GAO Code 351614). Detailed comments on the report recommendations are enclosed.

Sincerely,

Joseph K. Sikes
Director, Facilities Energy and Privatization

Enclosure:
As stated

GAO Draft Report Dated APRIL 2012
GAO-12-401 (GAO CODE 351614)

"RENEWABLE ENERGY PROJECT FINANCING: IMPROVED GUIDANCE AND
INFORMATION SHARING NEEDED FOR DOD PROJECT-LEVEL OFFICIALS"

DEPARTMENT OF DEFENSE COMMENTS
TO THE GAO RECOMMENDATIONS

RECOMMENDATION 1: The GAO recommends that the Secretary of Defense direct the
Under Secretary of Defense (Acquisition, Technology and Logistics), the Deputy Under
Secretary of Defense (Installations and Environment), and the military services to issue
comprehensive guidance that establishes and clearly describes the military services' processes to
ensure that business case analyses are completed and that these analyses fully consider the costs
and benefits of different financing approaches for renewable energy projects.

DoD RESPONSE: Partially Concur. The Department recognizes the importance of establishing
credible and effective guidance for energy project business case analyses for the military
services. However, the Department does not believe that a business case analysis must include
an analysis of all potential financing mechanisms. Certain authorities and their associated
financing strategies may not apply to certain renewable energy projects and an in-depth analysis
of their economic benefit would be unnecessary.

RECOMMENDATION 2: The GAO recommends that the Secretary of Defense direct the
Under Secretary of Defense (Acquisition, Technology and Logistics) and
the Deputy Under Secretary of Defense (Installations and Environment) to develop overarching
guidance about the use of available financing approaches for financing renewable energy
projects and direct the military services to update their guidance accordingly. At a minimum, this
guidance should include the requirements and restrictions of the underlying authorities and any
DOD-specific guidelines for using up-front appropriations and alternative financing approaches
for renewable energy projects.

DoD RESPONSE: Concur. The Department understands the importance of informing relevant
stakeholders of renewable energy project financing authorities and the benefits of their usage.
The Department expects to develop this comprehensive guidance that will include specific
authority requirements and restrictions and will discuss the variety of approaches and strategies
for financing renewable energy projects.

RECOMMENDATION 3: The GAO recommends that the Secretary of Defense direct the
Under Secretary of Defense (Acquisition, Technology and Logistics) and the Deputy Under
Secretary of Defense (Installations and Environment) to develop a formalized communications
process, such as a shared website or other appropriate approach, that will enable officials at
military installations to have timely access on an ongoing basis to information related to
financing renewable energy projects on other installations, including best practices and lessons

that other installations have learned from their experiences in financing their renewable energy projects.

DoD RESPONSE: Concur. The Department agrees that it is necessary to establish a more formalized communications method regarding the financing of renewable energy projects. This communication will enhance our ability to leverage best practices among our installations and personnel. The Office of the Deputy Under Secretary of Defense for Installations and Environment will be initiating an alternative financing energy working group with representatives from around the Department for this purpose.

Appendix V: GAO Contacts and Staff Acknowledgments

GAO Contacts	Brian J. Lepore, (202) 512-4523 or leporeb@gao.gov; or Frank Rusco, (202) 512-3841 or ruscof@gao.gov
Staff Acknowledgments	In addition to the contacts named above, Ernie Hazera, Assistant Director; Harold Reich, Assistant Director; Karyn Angulo; Hilary Benedict; Michael J. Hanson; Carol Henn; Charles Perdue; Mike Silver; Erik Wilkins-McKee; and Michael Willems made key contributions to this report.

Related GAO Products

Renewable Energy: Federal Agencies Implement Hundreds of Initiatives. GAO-12-260. Washington, D.C.: February 27, 2012.

Defense Infrastructure: DOD Did Not Fully Address the Supplemental Reporting Requirements in Its Energy Management Report. GAO-12-336R. Washington, D.C.: January 31, 2012.

Defense Infrastructure: Department of Defense Renewable Energy Initiatives. GAO-10-681R. Washington, D.C.: April 26, 2010.

Defense Infrastructure: DOD Needs to Take Actions to Address Challenges in Meeting Federal Renewable Energy Goals. GAO-10-104. Washington, D.C.: December 18, 2009.

Advanced Energy Technologies: Budget Trends and Challenges for DOE's Energy R&D Program. GAO-08-556T. Washington, D.C.: March 5, 2008.

Advanced Energy Technologies: Key Challenges to Their Development and Deployment. GAO-07-550T. Washington, D.C.: February 28, 2007.

Department of Energy: Key Challenges Remain for Developing and Deploying Advanced Energy Technologies to Meet Future Needs. GAO-07-106. Washington, D.C.: December 20, 2006.

Renewable Energy: Increased Geothermal Development Will Depend on Overcoming Many Challenges. GAO-06-629. Washington, D.C.: May 24, 2006.

Energy Savings: Performance Contracts Offer Benefits, but Vigilance Is Needed to Protect Government Interests. GAO-05-340. Washington, D.C.: June 22, 2005.

Meeting Energy Demand in the 21st Century: Many Challenges and Key Questions. GAO-05-414T. Washington, D.C.: March 16, 2005.

Capital Financing: Partnerships and Energy Savings Performance Contracts Raise Budgeting and Monitoring Concerns. GAO-05-55. Washington, D.C.: December 16, 2004.

Budget Issues: Alternative Approaches to Finance Federal Capital. GAO-03-1011. Washington, D.C.: August 21, 2003.

GAO's Mission	The Government Accountability Office, the audit, evaluation, and investigative arm of Congress, exists to support Congress in meeting its constitutional responsibilities and to help improve the performance and accountability of the federal government for the American people. GAO examines the use of public funds; evaluates federal programs and policies; and provides analyses, recommendations, and other assistance to help Congress make informed oversight, policy, and funding decisions. GAO's commitment to good government is reflected in its core values of accountability, integrity, and reliability.
Obtaining Copies of GAO Reports and Testimony	The fastest and easiest way to obtain copies of GAO documents at no cost is through GAO's website (www.gao.gov). Each weekday afternoon, GAO posts on its website newly released reports, testimony, and correspondence. To have GAO e-mail you a list of newly posted products, go to www.gao.gov and select "E-mail Updates."
Order by Phone	The price of each GAO publication reflects GAO's actual cost of production and distribution and depends on the number of pages in the publication and whether the publication is printed in color or black and white. Pricing and ordering information is posted on GAO's website, http://www.gao.gov/ordering.htm.
	Place orders by calling (202) 512-6000, toll free (866) 801-7077, or TDD (202) 512-2537.
	Orders may be paid for using American Express, Discover Card, MasterCard, Visa, check, or money order. Call for additional information.
Connect with GAO	Connect with GAO on Facebook, Flickr, Twitter, and YouTube. Subscribe to our RSS Feeds or E-mail Updates. Listen to our Podcasts. Visit GAO on the web at www.gao.gov.
To Report Fraud, Waste, and Abuse in Federal Programs	Contact: Website: www.gao.gov/fraudnet/fraudnet.htm E-mail: fraudnet@gao.gov Automated answering system: (800) 424-5454 or (202) 512-7470
Congressional Relations	Katherine Siggerud, Managing Director, siggerudk@gao.gov, (202) 512-4400, U.S. Government Accountability Office, 441 G Street NW, Room 7125, Washington, DC 20548
Public Affairs	Chuck Young, Managing Director, youngc1@gao.gov, (202) 512-4800 U.S. Government Accountability Office, 441 G Street NW, Room 7149 Washington, DC 20548